Grandad Paints

By Nora Henry

Library For All Ltd.

Grandad Paints

First published 2023

Published by Library For All Ltd
Email: info@libraryforall.org
URL: libraryforall.org

Our Yarning logo design by Jason Lee, Bidjipidji Art

Original illustrations by Clarice Masajo

Grandad Paints
Henry, Nora
ISBN: 978-1-923063-06-8
SKU03371

Grandad Paints

Nora lives in Kununurra and loves to visit her grandad at the art centre.

He loves teaching her and her son, Colton, about painting.

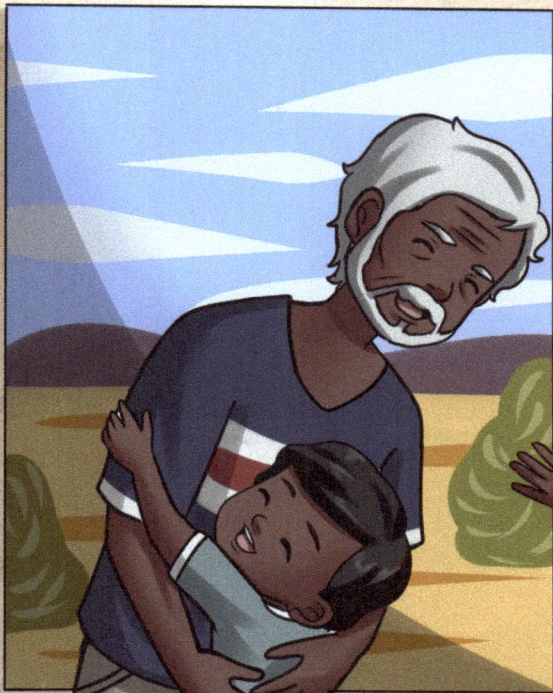

Colton always makes
a big mess.

Grandad is always patient and shows them many things about art and painting.

Grandad uses lots of colours to show the country and community of Police Hole.

Colton draws the house and the yard's dots near the swamp.

14

Nora paints the swamp, which has barra, turkey and other animals living there.

Police Hole has very high red cliffs and are near their house.

Nora and Colton love painting, visiting Grandad, and painting pictures of their community.

You can use these questions to talk about this book with your family, friends and teachers.

What did you learn from this book?

Describe this book in one word. Funny? Scary? Colourful? Interesting?

How did this book make you feel when you finished reading it?

What was your favourite part of this book?

download our reader app
getlibraryforall.org

About the author

Nora was born in Darwin and lives at Police Hole community. She loves going to the art centre with her son. They learn from her grandpa who is a famous artist. She loved hearing stories from her elders when she was young.

Author's Country

Darwin

OUR YARNING

NORTHERN
TERRITORY

QUEENSLAND

WESTERN
AUSTRALIA

SOUTH
AUSTRALIA

Brisbane

NEW SOUTH
WALES

Perth

Adelaide

Sydney

ACT
Canberra

VICTORIA
Melbourne

TASMANIA
Hobart

Our Yarning

Want to discover more books from this collection? Our Yarning is a collection of books written by Aboriginal and Torres Strait Islander peoples across Australia.

We know that children learn better, and enjoy reading more, when they see themselves in the stories, characters and illustrations of the books they read.

To download the app, visit the Google Play Store on any Android device and search 'Our Yarning'.

libraryforall.org

www.ingramcontent.com/pod-product-compliance
Lightning Source LLC
Chambersburg PA
CBHW042346040426
42448CB00019B/3432